LUCIA RUSH

Spaghetti Science

So you like spaghetti. But how much do you like spaghetti?

DID YOU KNOW THAT THERE IS A DAY WHEN THE WHOLE WORLD CELEBRATES SPAGHETTI?

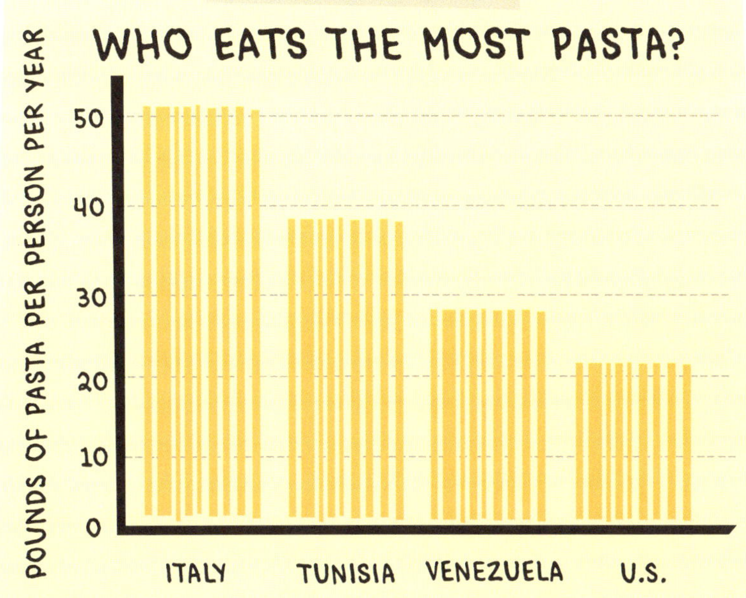

Do you like spaghetti a lot? Then maybe you are ready to learn all about spaghetti science!

But what is spaghetti science? I'm glad you asked. It is the science carried out by Spaghetti Scientists. These experts can:

AMAZE PEOPLE WITH SPAGHETTI TALK.

PUT ON SHOWS OF SPAGHETTI MAGIC.

WHISPER ASTONISHING SPAGHETTI SECRETS.

EXPLAIN COMPLICATED SPAGHETTI TECHNIQUES.

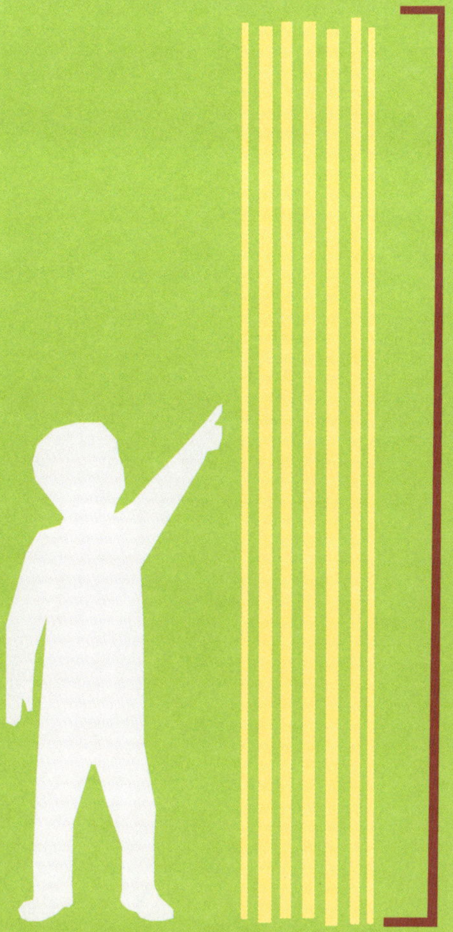

TELL TALL SPAGHETTI TALES.

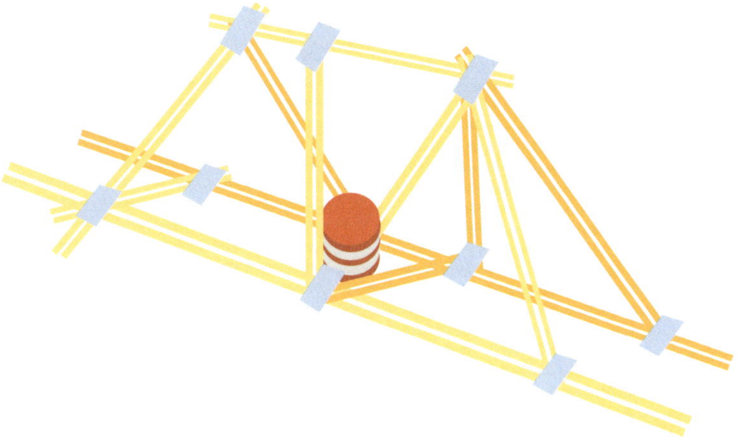

PERFORM FEATS OF SPAGHETTI SKILL.

AND MOST IMPORTANT OF ALL: COOK THE BEST SPAGHETTI ON EARTH!

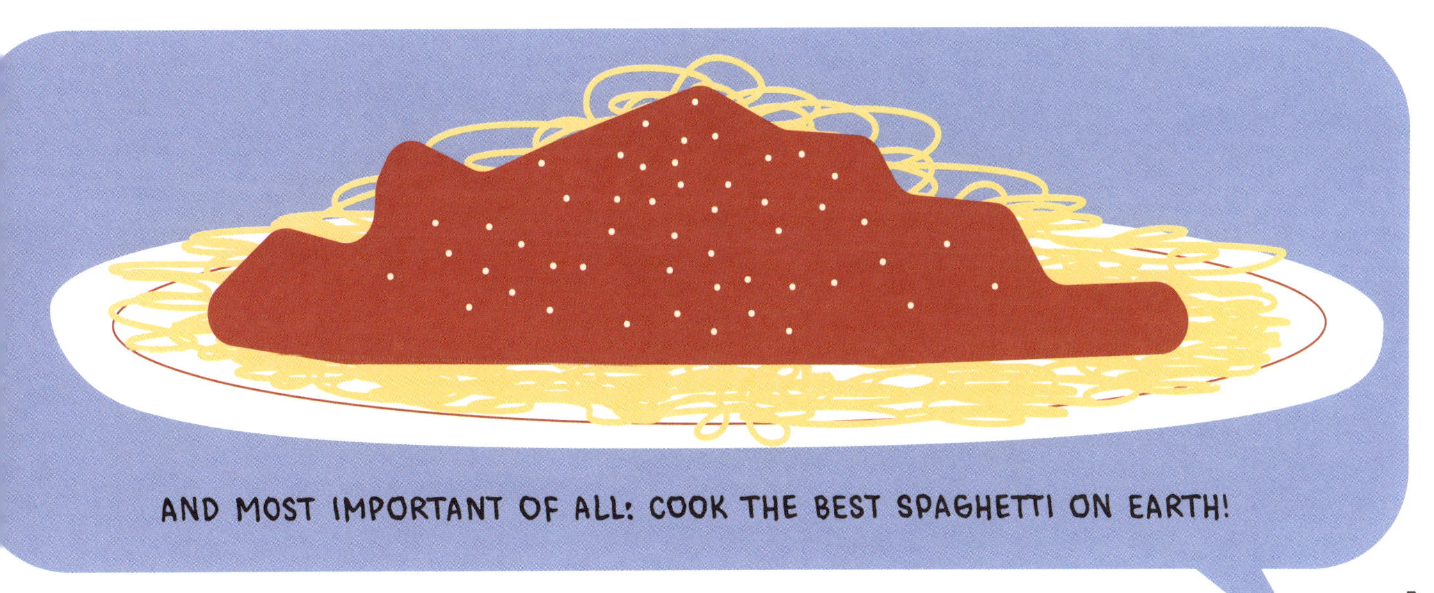

Now what is spaghetti? Well...

THIS IS NOT SPAGHETTI. THIS IS RAMEN: A THIN AND WAVY NOODLE, OFTEN FLOATING IN A FLAVORFUL BROTH WITH TASTY TOPPINGS LIKE EGGS, VEGGIES, AND SEAWEED!

THIS IS NOT SPAGHETTI. THIS IS SPÄTZLE: SQUIGGLY, EGGY NOODLES MADE BY DROPPING DOUGH INTO BOILING WATER! WHEN YOU COVER THEM IN MELTY CHEESE, YOU CREATE KÄSESPÄTZLE, A CHEESY DREAM!

THIS IS NOT SPAGHETTI. THIS IS FIDEO: TINY NOODLES WITH A BIG JOB! IN SPAIN, IT SWIMS IN SEAFOOD DISHES. IN MEXICO, IT DIVES INTO A TOMATOEY SOUP TO CREATE A WARM HUG IN A BOWL!

THIS IS NOT SPAGHETTI. THIS IS LO MEIN: LONG, SLURPABLE NOODLES TOSSED IN A YUMMY, SALTY SAUCE! JUST MIX THEM UP WITH SOME VEGGIES, MEAT, AND A DRIZZLE OF SOY SAUCE!

THIS IS SPAGHETTI! OUR FAVORITE LONG, SWIRLY NOODLE DISH. THIS ONE IS TOPPED WITH TANGY TOMATO SAUCE AND A SPRINKLE OF SALTY CHEESE CALLED PARMESAN.

Let's take a closer look!

Out in the countryside, there are fields and fields of golden wheat swaying in the breeze. This special wheat is called durum wheat. Each stalk holds tiny, hard grains. These grains hold the secret to making our favorite dish...spaghetti!

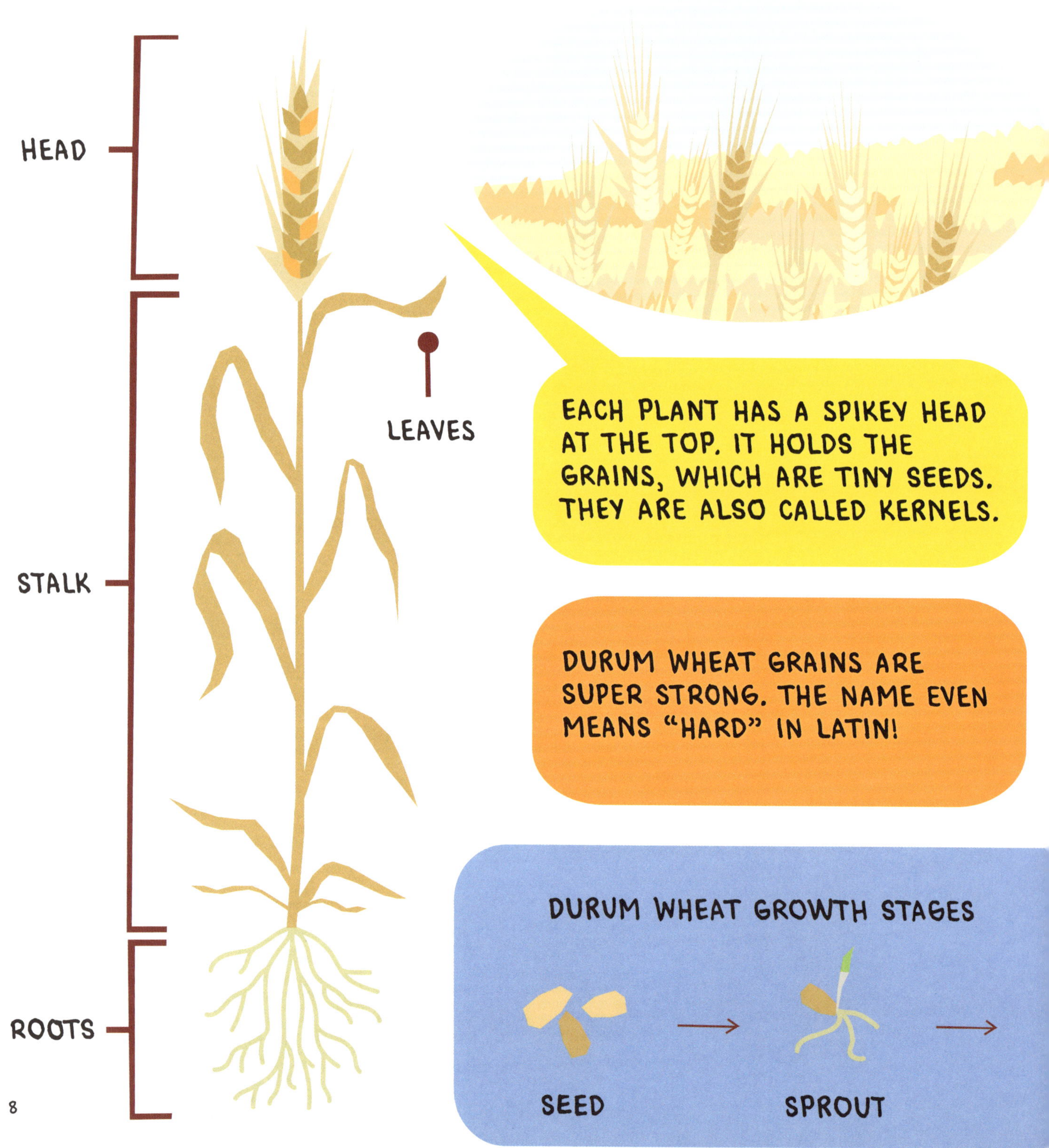

Once the wheat reaches the perfect shade of golden brown, farmers collect the plants—a process called harvesting. Traditionally, farmers did this by hand. They used sickles to cut the wheat, and then they beat the stalks to shake out the grains, and then they bagged it up. In some places, it is still done this way.

Today, harvesting is still done in 3 steps. But it is often carried out with the help of special machines called combine harvesters.

1

REAPING

WHEAT STALKS ARE CUT FROM THE GROUND

2

THRESHING

THE KERNELS ARE SEPARATED FROM THE REST OF THE PLANT

3

BAGGING AND HAULING

THE GRAIN IS COLLECTED AND DRIVEN OFF THE FIELD

A COMBINE HARVESTER CAN HARVEST ENOUGH WHEAT IN A DAY TO MAKE HUNDREDS OF THOUSANDS OF PLATES OF SPAGHETTI!

THAT'S ENOUGH TO FEED A WHOLE CITY THE SIZE OF FLORENCE, ITALY!

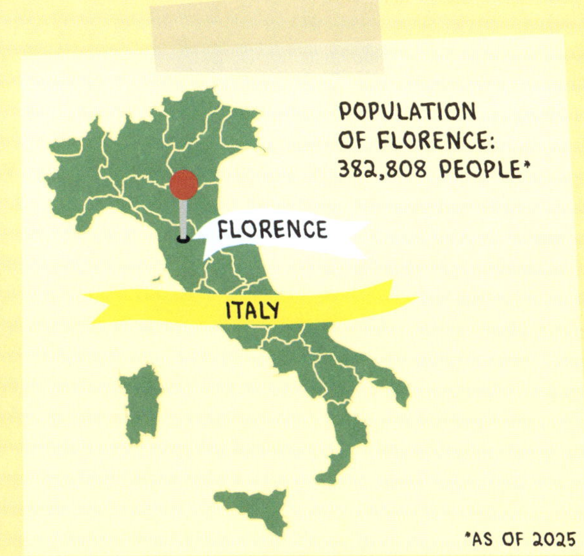

1

2

3

The harvested durum wheat grains are brought to the factory for their big transformation into semolina flour, through a process called milling. Unlike regular wheat, which produces fine flour, durum wheat breaks into coarse particles, which is perfect for pasta because it gives it its famous chew!

ROLLER MILLS
FLOUR OUTLET
FLOUR MILL
SEMOLINA FLOUR
THE WHEAT GOES THROUGH UP TO 10 DIFFERENT SETS OF ROLLERS BEFORE THE MILLING IS DONE!

The flour is mixed with water and...ta-da! We have dough! Unlike bread dough, pasta dough has very little water, usually around 3 parts water to 7 parts flour, which helps keep it firm and not sticky. This makes the perfect chewy spaghetti!

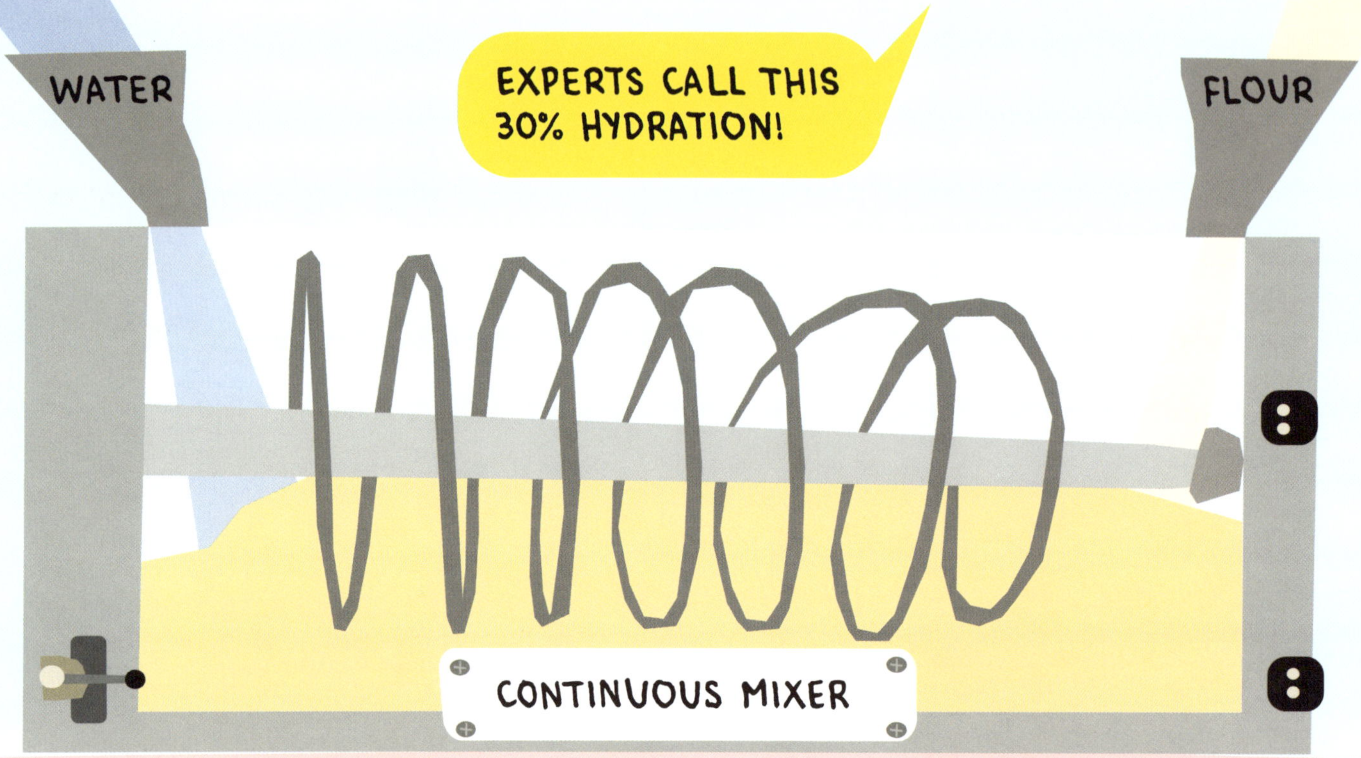

WATER

EXPERTS CALL THIS 30% HYDRATION!

FLOUR

CONTINUOUS MIXER

Now the dough is kneaded to perfection, and a very important element in the magic of spaghetti comes into play—gluten!

GLUTEN IS THE STRETCHY PART OF WHEAT. WHEN YOU MIX FLOUR WITH WATER AND KNEAD IT, GLUTEN ACTS LIKE GLUE THAT HOLDS EVERYTHING TOGETHER, MAKING IT STRONG AND BENDY.

BUT SOME PEOPLE'S TUMMIES REACT BADLY TO GLUTEN. LUCKILY THERE IS SPECIAL PASTA FOR THEM MADE FROM RICE, CHICKPEAS, OR EVEN LENTILS!

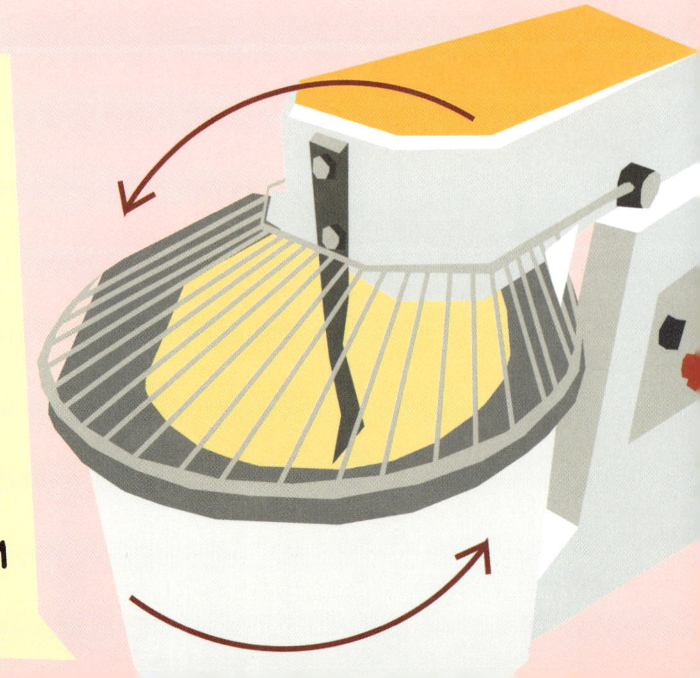

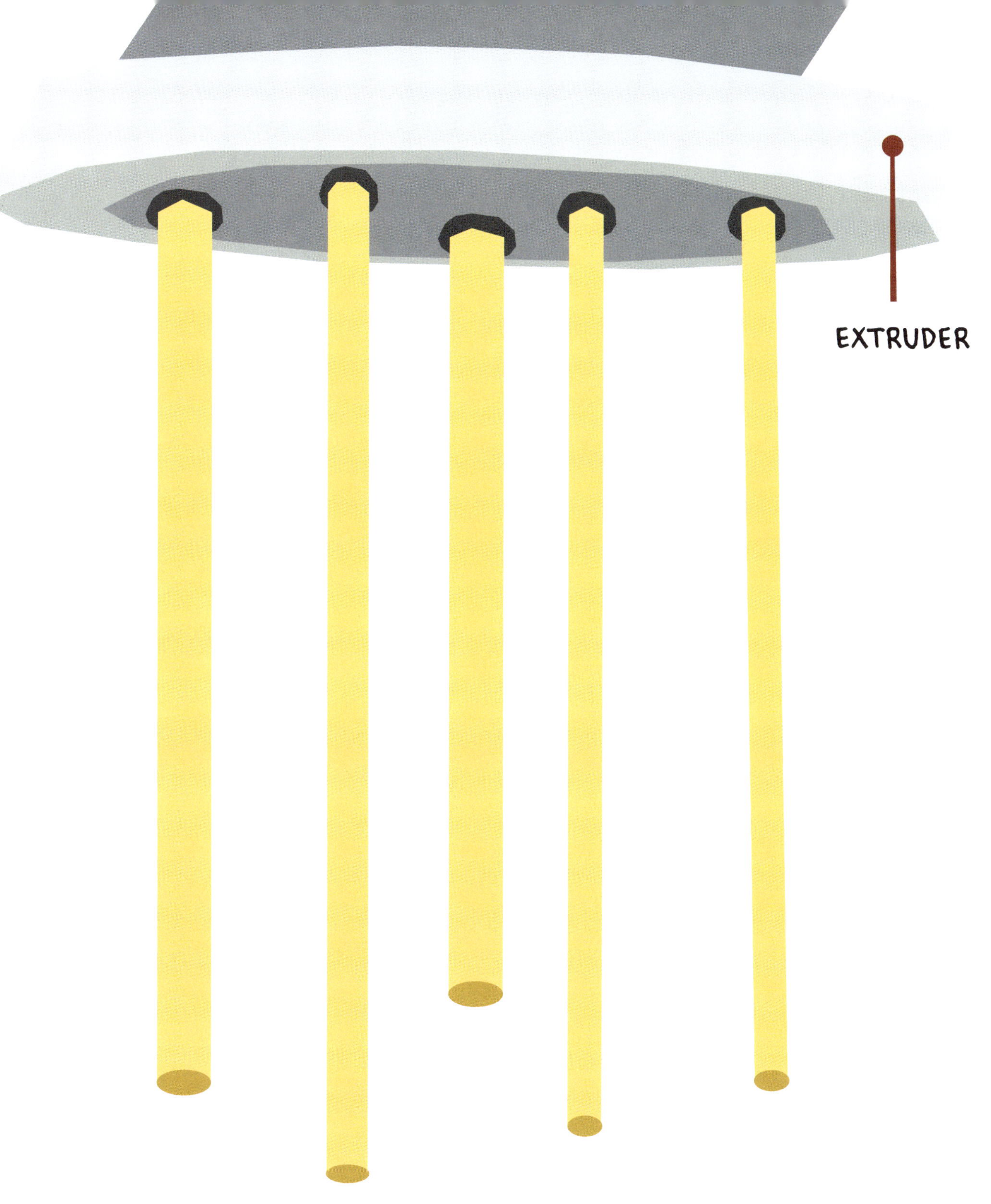

Now, the real magic happens when the dough is made into long edible noodles through a process called extrusion, during which the dough is pressed through special metal molds called dies. But don't be frightened, it's not as scary as it sounds!

The noodles are carefully and slowly dried for several hours, sprinkled with semolina flour so they don't stick together, cut into 10-inch (25.5-centimeter) pieces, portioned, and finally dressed up into packages.

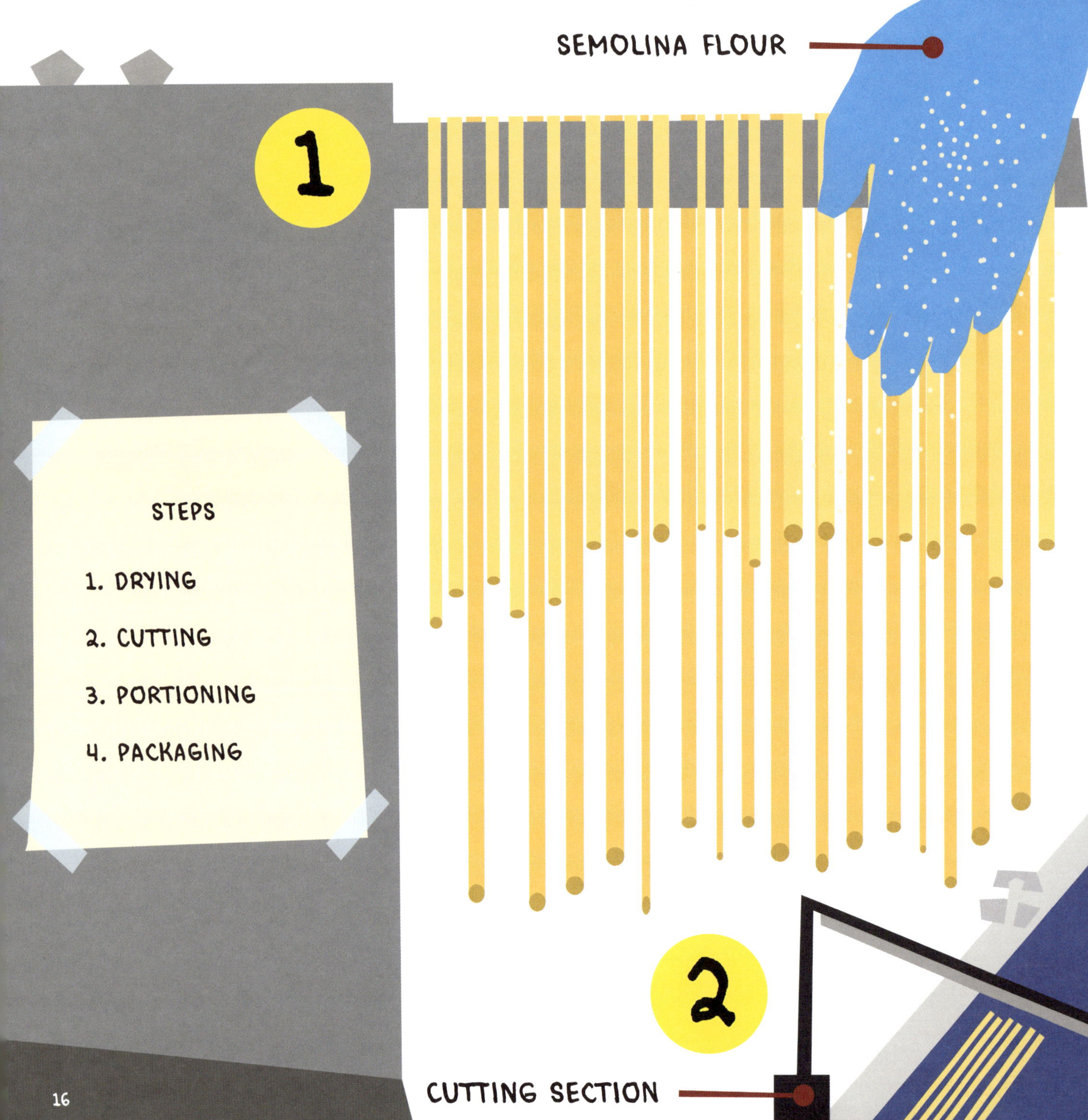

The dried and cut spaghetti travels on long, vibrating conveyor belts that keep the strands from sticking together before being packaged.

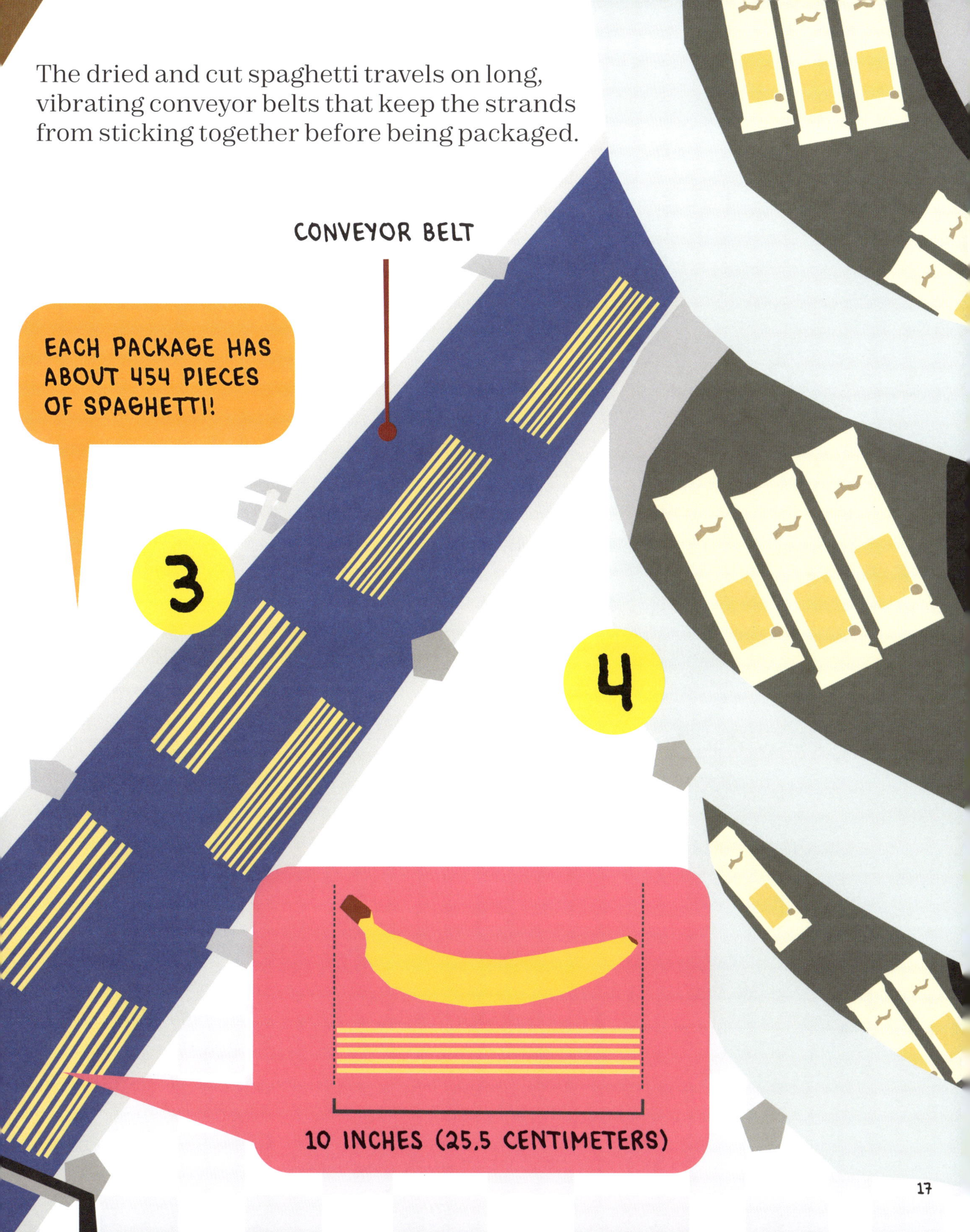

Spaghetti is packed in plastic bags or cardboard boxes. Most of them even have see-through windows so you can see the pasta inside and pick your favorite one!

Now that the spaghetti is dressed up in packaging, it can be free to begin its grand adventure around the world to reach the supermarkets!

Take a walk down the pasta aisle and become a spaghetti detective! Look closely...what differences do you see?

WHAT TO LOOK FOR:

SEE ANY SPAGHETTI THAT LOOKS A LITTLE ROUGH AND PALE? THAT'S A GOOD SIGN! IT WAS PROBABLY MADE WITH BRONZE DIES, WHICH ARE SPECIAL MOLDS THAT GIVE THE NOODLES A ROUGH SURFACE. WHY? BECAUSE SAUCE STICKS BETTER AND IT HAS A YUMMIER, CHEWIER BITE!

Trucks rumble down the roads, carrying packages of spaghetti to local stores. Trains chug along, transporting large quantities of spaghetti across countries.

Ships sail across oceans, bringing spaghetti to faraway lands, and airplanes soar through the sky, delivering spaghetti everywhere.

STOP

The spaghetti waits patiently on the shelves for you to take it home and cook your favorite dish!

SPAGHETTI HAS A SHELF LIFE OF 1 TO 2 YEARS, THANKS TO HOW IT'S MADE AND PACKAGED.

DRY PASTA IS MADE WITHOUT EGGS AND HAS ALMOST NO MOISTURE, WHICH MEANS BACTERIA STAYS AWAY!

Pasta comes in all shapes and sizes! From the classic long strands to spirals and twists, each one has its own name, birthplace, and personality.

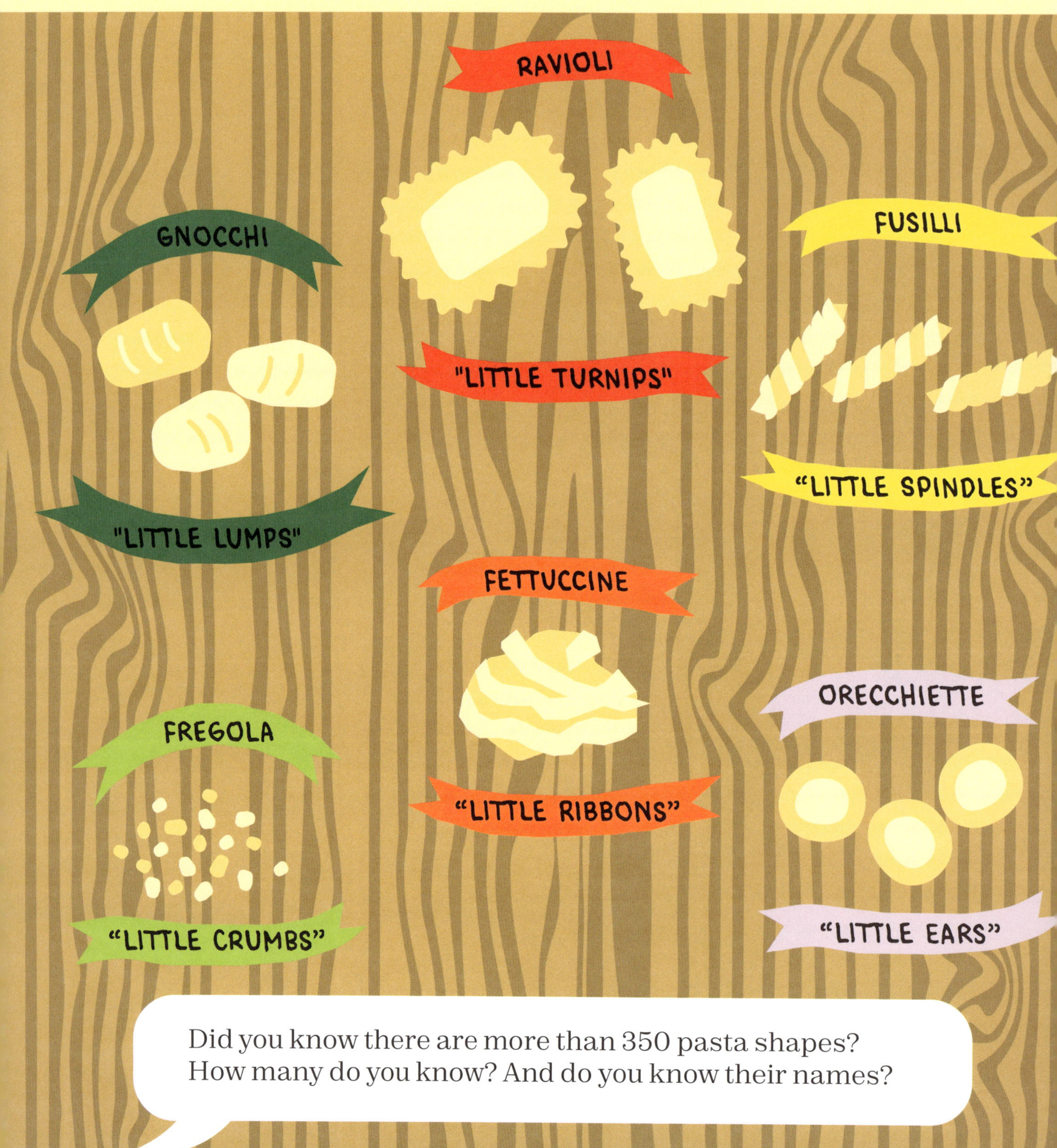

ITALY
TRENTINO ALTO ADIGE
FRIULI VENEZIA GIULIA
VALLE D'AOSTA
LOMBARDIA
VENETO
PIEMONTE
LIGURIA
EMILIA ROMAGNA
TOSCANA
MARCHE
UMBRIA
ABRUZZO
LAZIO
MOLISE
CAMPANIA
PUGLIA
SARDEGNA
BASILICATA
CALABRIA
SICILIA
THE HOME OF...
GNOCCHI
RAVIOLI
FUSILLI
FREGOLA
FETTUCCINE
ORECCHIETTE
SPAGHETTI!!!!
THIS IS NAPLES! IT IS KNOWN AS THE PASTA CAPITAL OF ITALY BECAUSE OF ITS PERFECT DRYING CLIMATE!
AND HERE, ON THE SUNNY, TRIANGULAR ISLAND OF SICILY, IS THE BIRTHPLACE OF ONE OF THE GREATEST INVENTIONS IN HUMAN HISTORY... SPAGHETTI!
DID YOU KNOW THAT THE FIRST INDUSTRIAL PASTA FACTORY OPENED IN VENICE IN 1740?
THAT'S OLDER THAN...
• THE UNITED STATES! (FOUNDED IN 1776)
• THE INVENTION OF THE BICYCLE! (INVENTED IN 1817)
• THE FIRST PHOTOGRAPH! (TAKEN IN 1826)

Now I am going to let you in on some of the world's best spaghetti secrets.

EVERY TIME YOU SAY SPAGHETTI, YOU SPEAK ITALIAN. SPAGO MEANS "STRING," SO EVERY TIME YOU SAY "CAN I HAVE A BOWL OF SPAGHETTI?" YOU ARE ACTUALLY SAYING:

"CAN I HAVE A BOWL OF LITTLE STRINGS?"

THE WORLD'S LARGEST PORTION OF SPAGHETTI WAS SO BIG THAT IT FILLED AN ENTIRE SWIMMING POOL!

ITALIANS EAT SO MUCH SPAGHETTI THAT IN ONE YEAR IT WOULD BE ENOUGH TO WRAP AROUND THE WORLD 15,000 TIMES.

ITALY MAKES THE MOST PASTA. IT SELLS AROUND 2.2 MILLION TONS EVERY YEAR TO OTHER COUNTRIES.

THAT IS ABOUT THE SAME WEIGHT AS:

FLOUR
EGGS
SALT
1
2
3
10
4
60

Now it's your turn! Grab a grown-up helper and get ready. It's time to get your hands floury!

HOW TO MAKE HOMEMADE SPAGHETTI:

INGREDIENTS

FOR 2 SERVINGS:

2 EGGS

1 2/3 CUPS
(200 GRAMS) FLOUR

A PINCH OF SALT

STEPS

1. **MAKE A FLOUR MOUNTAIN:**
   POUR THE FLOUR ONTO A CLEAN COUNTER AND USE YOUR HANDS TO MAKE A HOLE IN THE MIDDLE.
2. **CRACK & MIX:**
   CRACK THE EGGS INTO THE HOLE, SPRINKLE IN THE SALT, AND USE A FORK TO GENTLY MIX THE EGGS, SLOWLY PULLING IN FLOUR FROM THE SIDES UNTIL IT IS ALL MIXED TOGETHER.
3. **KNEAD, KNEAD, KNEAD:**
   NOW USE YOUR HANDS TO MUSH THE DOUGH FOR ABOUT 10 MINUTES, UNTIL IT FORMS A NICE BALL.
4. **LET IT REST:**
   WRAP YOUR DOUGH IN PLASTIC WRAP AND LET IT REST FOR 1 HOUR. THIS HELPS MAKE IT STRETCHY!
5. **ROLL & CUT:**
   FINALLY, SPRINKLE SOME FLOUR ON YOUR SURFACE SO THE DOUGH DOESN'T STICK. ROLL IT OUT AS THIN AS YOU LIKE, THEN CAREFULLY CUT IT INTO SKINNY STRIPS WITH A KNIFE.

FRESH PASTA DOUGH IS TASTIEST WHEN COOKED AND EATEN RIGHT AWAY.

IT IS ALSO DONE COOKING IN ONLY 1–3 MINUTES!

It's time to cook the spaghetti to perfection! Now get armed with your utensils and essentials:

ROMA
SALT
DICED TOMATOES
SUGAR
OLIVE OIL
PARMESAN
YOUR FAVORITE SPAGHETTI OR HOMEMADE SPAGHETTI

Bravo, chef! Now it's time for the next delicious step: bringing it all together in a tasty sauce. Ready for level two?

HOW TO MAKE SPAGHETTI AL POMODORO (SPAGHETTI WITH TOMATO SAUCE)

INGREDIENTS

FOR 2 SERVINGS:

7 OUNCES (200 GRAMS) SPAGHETTI

3 TABLESPOONS OLIVE OIL

1 CAN (14 OUNCES/ 400 GRAMS) DICED TOMATOES

SALT

1 TEASPOON OF SUGAR

PARMESAN, AS MUCH AS YOU LIKE!

STEPS

1. FILL A MEDIUM-SIZED POT HALFWAY WITH WATER, ADD A PINCH OF SALT, COVER, AND BRING TO A BOIL.
2. GRATE AS MUCH PARMESAN AS YOU LIKE INTO A LITTLE MOUND AND SET ASIDE.
3. ADD THE SPAGHETTI TO THE BOILING WATER AND COOK UNTIL AL DENTE. (HMM...LET'S LEARN MORE ABOUT THIS WORD SOON!)
4. MEANWHILE, HEAT YOUR FRYING PAN OVER MEDIUM HEAT AND ADD THE OLIVE OIL, DICED TOMATOES, SALT, AND SUGAR.
5. DRAIN THE SPAGHETTI IN A COLANDER OVER THE SINK.
6. ADD THE SPAGHETTI TO THE PAN WITH THE SAUCE AND STIR.
7. SCOOP THE SPAGHETTI ONTO YOUR PLATE, TOP WITH A LITTLE MOUNTAIN OF PARMESAN, AND ENJOY!

Ready to get started? Continue reading to learn all the details!

First fill the pot halfway with water and a pinch of salt. Cover with a lid, turn the heat up all the way, and let the water come to a boil.

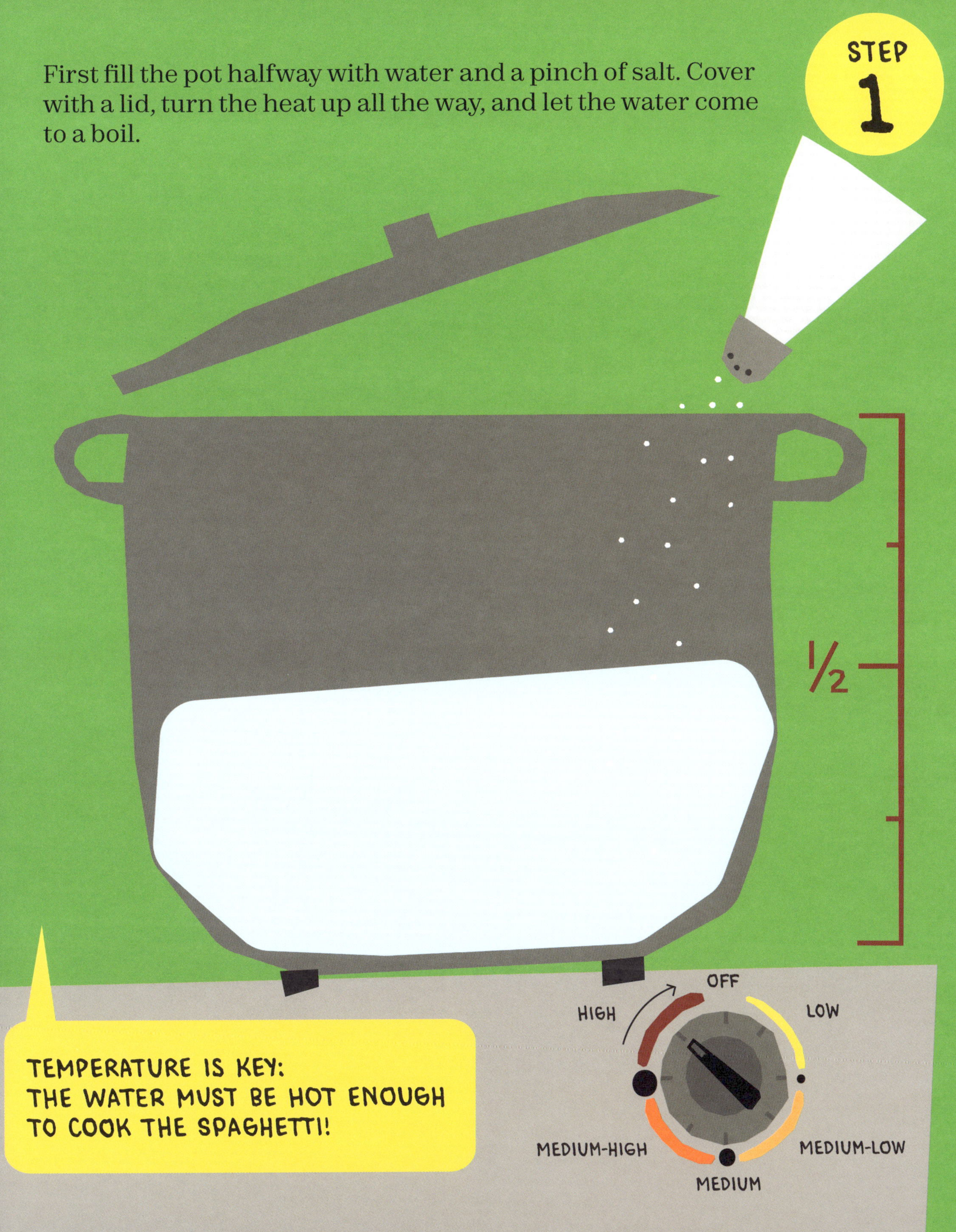

STEP 2

While the water is heating up, grab the parmesan and carefully grate it until you have a little mountain of cheese. Save this for later.

STEP 3

Now let's go back to the pot. Once the water is boiling, add the spaghetti to the pot and turn it down to medium heat.

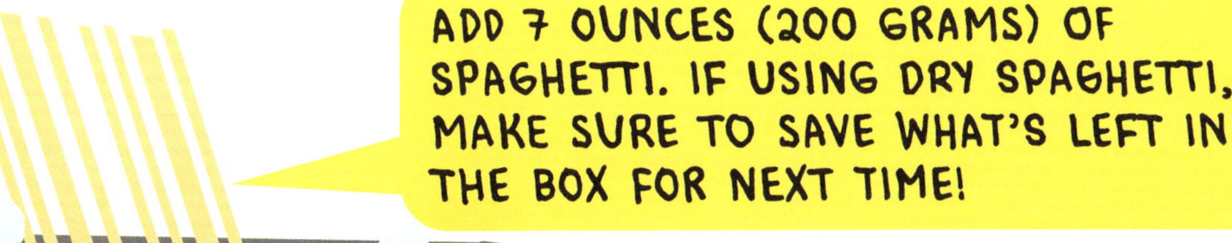

WATER BOILS WHEN IT HITS 212°F (100°C). THAT IS HOT ENOUGH TO TURN WATER INTO STEAM! THOSE BUBBLES MEAN THE MOLECULES ARE MOVING FAST AND ESCAPING AS GAS. SPAGHETTI NEEDS THIS HEAT TO COOK JUST RIGHT.

Watch the water bubble and the spaghetti noodles dance inside the pot as they cook.

In about 8 10 minutes, they'll be ready. (Or 2–3 if you are using homemade spaghetti.)

While they boil, let's get a head start on the sauce!

While the spaghetti is dancing in the pot, turn your frying pan to medium heat, and add:

Let this cook on medium heat for 20 minutes.

These are roma tomatoes in a can, and they are perfect for the job. These tomatoes have a firm flesh, and few seeds, and they are less watery than their other tomato friends, making them full of flavor!

There are over 10,000 kinds of tomatoes in the world! They can be big or small, round or oval, red, yellow, green, and even purple!

Tomatoes are very special. While most fruits and vegetables have just one or two of the five basic tastes, tomatoes have four!

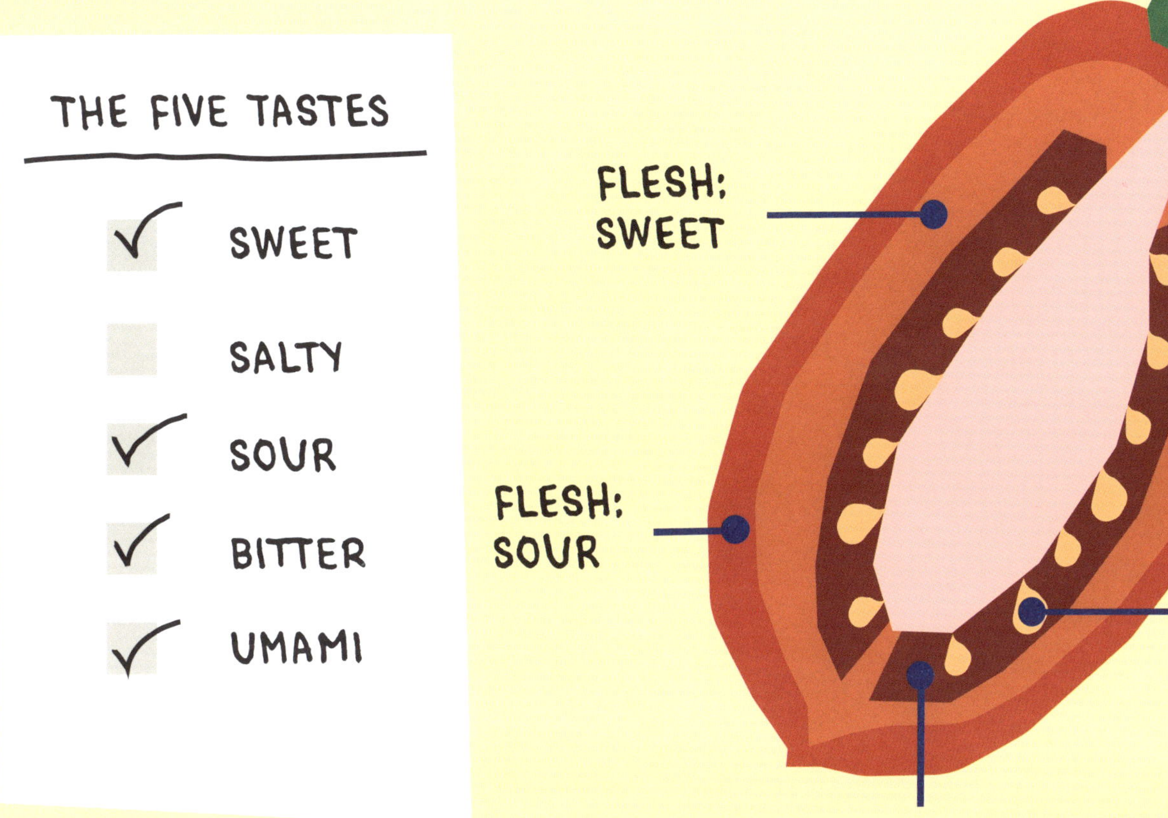

Fun fact: Italy's Mount Vesuvius is a volcano, and it helps grow some of the world's best tomatoes, like the Piennolo! The soil is full of minerals that make them extra sweet, and juicy—great tomatoes for spaghetti sauce!

Now back to the spaghetti! How do we know when it's ready? It has to be "al dente." Let's start testing one minute before the cooking time is up!

"Al dente" (say: ahl-DEN-teh!) is the Italian way of saying pasta is cooked just right—not too soft, not too hard, but perfectly chewy!

"Al dente" means "to the tooth" in Italian.

SPAGHETTI TESTS

THE BITE TEST:

GRAB A NOODLE AND TAKE A TINY BITE. IT SHOULD BE SOFT ON THE OUTSIDE BUT HAVE A LITTLE CHEW IN THE MIDDLE.

THE STICK TEST:

SOME CHEFS EVEN THROW A NOODLE AT THE WALL, AND IF IT STICKS, IT'S READY TO EAT!

TRY IT YOURSELF!

Once the spaghetti is ready, turn off the stove and pour the spaghetti into the colander, over the sink, so the water swims down the drain.

STEP 6

Add the spaghetti to the sauce and mix it around with the wooden spoon until everything is nicely combined.

THE TEASPOON OF SUGAR ADDS A TOUCH OF SWEETNESS TOO!

NOW THAT WE'VE COOKED DOWN THE TOMATOES INTO A SAUCE, THE HEAT HAS UNLOCKED THEIR NATURAL SWEETNESS.

THAT'S BECAUSE THE HEAT BREAKS DOWN THE ACIDS IN THE TOMATOES AND BRINGS OUT THEIR NATURAL SUGARS!

STEP 7

Now plate your finished dish, with a sea of spaghetti and a little mountain of cheese on top.

And finally, grab your fork, and maybe a spoon or a knife too, and twirl!

HOW TO TWIRL: USE YOUR FORK TO CATCH SOME SPAGHETTI, THEN SPIN IT UNTIL THE STRANDS ARE PERFECTLY WOUND UP.

Spaghetti isn't just delicious, it's also perfect for science experiments and fascinating physics tests.

MISSION: SPAGHETTI BRIDGE!

- GRAB SOME DRY SPAGHETTI AND TWO STURDY BOOKS.
- NOW, TAPE THE NOODLES SIDE BY SIDE TO MAKE THE BRIDGE STRONG, AND START BUILDING UPWARDS! ONCE YOUR BRIDGE IS READY... IT'S TIME TO TEST IT! PLACE COINS ONE BY ONE ONTO YOUR BRIDGE.
- TEST HOW MANY COINS YOUR BRIDGE CAN HOLD BEFORE IT BREAKS!

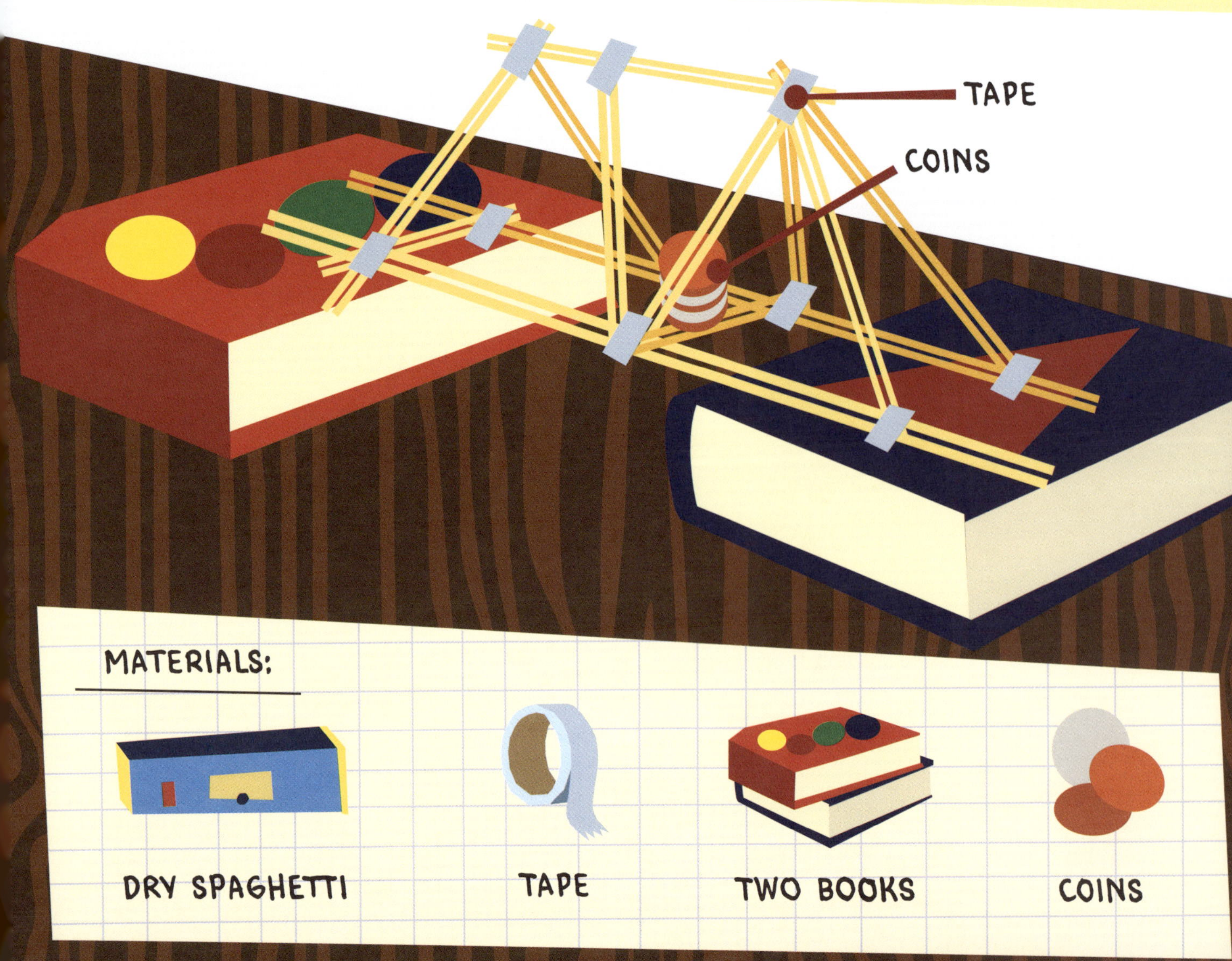

Why does a dry spaghetti noodle always break into three or more pieces instead of two when you bend it?

Test it yourself! This physics problem has actually puzzled scientists for decades. Here's how it works:

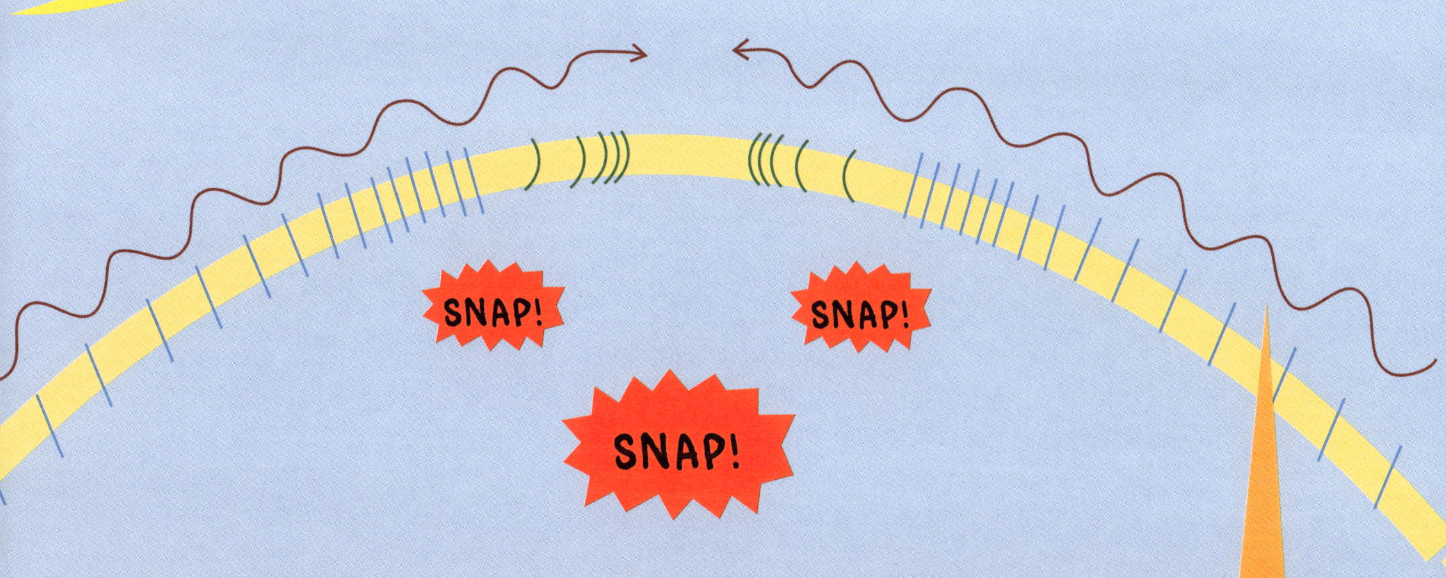

Bending causes the first break, and that break releases energy as a vibrational wave that travels through the noodle, bending it again and causing more breaks!

Spaghetti can be prepared in so many different ways! Do you see your favorite?

SPAGHETTI AL PESTO

SPAGHETTI AGLIO E OLIO

SPAGHETTI CON POLPETTE

MENU

SPAGHETTI AL PESTO..VEGETARIAN
SPAGHETTI WITH PESTO MADE FROM FRESH BASIL, GARLIC, PINE NUTS, PARMESAN, AND OLIVE OIL

SPAGHETTI CON POLPETTE......................................WITH MEAT
SPAGHETTI WITH MEATBALLS, TOMATO SAUCE, AND PARMESAN

SPAGHETTI AGLIO E OLIO..VEGAN
SPAGHETTI WITH GARLIC, OLIVE OIL, RED PEPPER FLAKES, AND FRESH PARSLEY

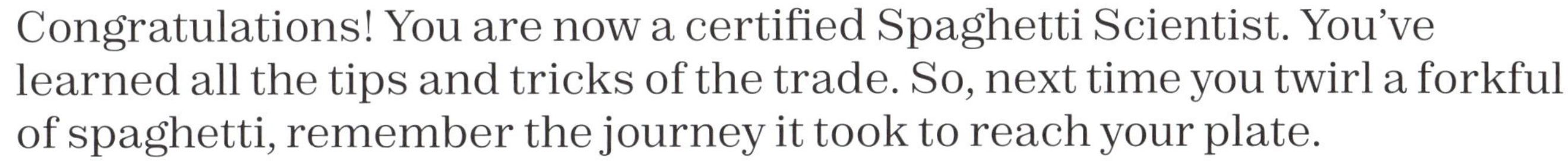

Congratulations! You are now a certified Spaghetti Scientist. You've learned all the tips and tricks of the trade. So, next time you twirl a forkful of spaghetti, remember the journey it took to reach your plate.

CERTIFIED SPAGHETTI SCIENTIST

YOUR CERTIFICATE IS READY.
DOWNLOAD IT HERE!

Thank you to my inspiring parents for teaching me to love cooking and for all the fun we have playing around in the kitchen.

— LUCIA

HELVETIQ publishing has been supported by the Swiss Federal Office of Culture with a structural grant for the years 2026–2028.

Spaghetti Science

Typesetting and layout: Lucia Rush
Cover design: Lucia Rush & Ajša Zdravković

ISBN: 978-3-03964-115-4
First edition: 2026
Printed in China

Mittlere Strasse 4
4056 Basel
Switzerland

helvetiq.com